The Scottish Football Annual No 1

The Scottish Football Annual No 1

Edited by Ian Archer

Stanley Paul

London   Melbourne   Sydney   Auckland   Johannesburg

Stanley Paul & Co. Ltd

An imprint of the Hutchinson Publishing Group

17–21 Conway Street, London W1P 6JD

Hutchinson Publishing Group (Australia) Pty Ltd
PO Box 496, 16–22 Church Street, Hawthorne, Melbourne, Victoria 3122
PO Box 151, Broadway, New South Wales 2007

Hutchinson Group (NZ) Ltd
32–34 View Road, PO Box 40–086, Glenfield, Auckland 10

Hutchinson Group (SA) Pty Ltd
PO Box 337, Bergvlei 2012, South Africa

First published 1984
© Stanley Paul & Co. Ltd 1984

Set in Linotron Baskerville by Wyvern Typesetting Limited, Bristol

Printed in Great Britain by
Butler & Tanner Ltd, Frome and London

ISBN 0 09 158901 0

Colour and black and white photographs by courtesy of Sportapics and Colorsport

Frontispiece:

Davie Provan in Celtic's 1–0 win in the Scottish League Cup semi-final
which halted the Dons' Treble bid

CONTENTS

Gordon Strachan, Willie Miller and Neil Simpson salute the Aberdeen fans after their Supercup triumph over Hamburg

HELLO AND WELCOME

Reports of the death of Scottish football were, once again this season, decidedly premature. If I had a pound note for every time someone has said that the game is dying, then I'd be able to buy Diego Maradona for my local club. But the game lives on in a vigorous state of health.

You won't hear them moaning at Aberdeen. Rangers can still pull in the fans. Dundee United and Celtic may have had seasons which they would prefer to forget. But in any case football is not just about the big four. It's about the few hundred unsung professionals who keep the game alive at grounds all over the country. It's about the Juniors, who stir up local passions in their towns and villages. It's about the juveniles and amateurs, young and old, good bad or indifferent who run about like ants on all those public pitches week in and week out. They are all having the time of their lives.

One abiding memory this season was going to Clydebank. Kilbowie Park is not one of the most fashionable places in the world – yet the club once made its entry into the Premier League, a feat which must rank at the top of the list of making daydreams come true and one which wasn't given the credit due at the time. Now they are in the middle order of Scottish football, which is still a credit to them. Clydebank happened to lose that day but here still was a side which was playing attractive football with the likes of Gerry McCabe and Gerry Ronald putting their feet on the ball and trying to bring out all those good Scottish qualities of cheeky arrogance. Sitting watching it were the Steedman brothers, looking at the game appreciatively at a ground where everyone sits down and where the paint, even at the end of a season, looked nice and fresh. That nice afternoon, with a seemingly endless supply of tea and sausage rolls at the end of it, seemed to sum up the true spirit of Scottish football.

Another memory was right at the start of the season when I went to see a brand new football club reborn. The little village of Stoneyburn, where the great Tommy Walker played his first games, decided it was time, after a lengthy absence, that they

Above: The faces of the future – Scotland's Professional Youth Squad, 1984

Opposite above: Aberdeen's first goal in the Supercup final, scored by Neil Simpson

Opposite below: Scotland's best performance in a poor season was their 2–0 win over Uruguay. Paul McStay breaks clear from Acevedo and de los Santos

reformed their defunct Junior Club. They built a pavilion, they cared for the pitch and on the great day, none other than the Scottish Junior Cup holders East Kilbride Thistle came down to play them. Why, they even brought the Cup itself with them and dads brought their young sons just to touch it. The sides sat down to a smashing steak-pie dinner afterwards. Whoever says football is dying isn't seeing the same game as this man.

That is not to say that everything's right with the game. Scotland itself had a disappointing season on the whole, with manager Jock Stein admitting at one stage that his team was in a rut. But really, it was almost to be expected with an early exit from the European Championship and the World Cup still over the horizon. Once the qualifying matches for Mexico are underway, the old adrenalin will return and we have too many good young

Opposite: John Hewitt, whose goal clinched the European Cup Winners' Cup the previous season, could not command a regular Aberdeen place. But he was in the side which beat Hamburg to win the Supercup

Above: Coasters, the Falkirk arena which was the scene of Tennent's Super Sixes, indoor football – with snow on the ground outside

players to regard those contests with anything other than soundly-based optimism.

The most worrying feature, as SFA secretary Ernie Walker will doubtless point out in his annual report, was indiscipline – and not only amongst the players. The Criminal Justice Act (Scotland) has brought a new atmosphere to the now sober terraces. Crowd trouble is increasingly associated with grounds south of the border although the need for vigilance remains eternal. But in the dug-outs and sometimes on the pitch, they were doing things for which the customer, had he perpetrated the same acts, would find himself under arrest. It was almost symbolic that a player was sent off in the Scottish Cup final for the first time since 1929.

The game at the top is getting too overheated. And every car owner will tell you that when the radiator temperature rises above a certain level, only one thing can happen. It explodes. For this, the managers must take some of the blame. I know theirs is a

11

difficult, maybe even an impossible, task – but winning at all costs was never a central part of football philosophy. Dundee United's Jim McLean was fined £500, banned from the touchline and lost his job as Stein's assistant following one outburst and I really do think we have a right to expect better behaviour than we get in some dug-outs.

Tommy Docherty always says that whatever else a manager may do, when the players cross the touchline they are on their own – and the manager may as well just go home. A typical piece of hyperbole from the Doc, but it does contain an element of truth. Personally, I wouldn't mind seeing an SFA rule which limits the number of people in any given dug-out to three – two subs and the sponge man. Managers could then sit in the stand and give fresh advice only in the dressing-room at the interval. Players rarely hear much of the bawling and shouting which goes on. And referees, carrying out a thankless task, deserve some consideration.

But that apart it was another splendid season. My thanks go, almost entirely, to the players who have entertained me. But also to those officials, directors, managers and all the others around Scotland's football grounds who are mostly ready to give one a cheery greeting. Football is about friendship as much as anything else – and in that instance I'm a richer man at the end of it.

Supersub Eric Black of Aberdeen

MEXICO, HERE WE COME?

Alex McLeish made a joke about it. Cimbing on board the flight that was to carry Scotland's squad out of Marseilles and home to Abbotsinch after the match against France, he said: 'They were good weren't they. I enjoyed watching them.' The 2–0 defeat against a team which could be called the Brazilians of Europe brought to a close an international season which could only be described as disappointing.

Of the seven games played, only two – against Uruguay and Wales – were won. It hardly seemed the ideal way to prepare for the next World Cup but as manager Jock Stein left for his summer holidays he was more optimistic than downhearted that Scotland could again navigate itself through the qualifying waters to come home safely to shore in Mexico. Only the downright foolish would beg to disagree with him.

'We always seem to have a slump between World Cups. We've never really made a go of the European Championships. I'd be the first to admit that the season was a disappointment to the fans. And believe me it was an even bigger disappointment to the players and myself. But that is in the past. From now on, we have to sort out our best squad for the qualifying matches and if we play as well as I am convinced we can, we should qualify,' he said.

That was a clarion call as those matches against Iceland, Wales and Spain beckoned and Scotland girded its loins to make sure that the successive triumphs in qualifying for West Germany, Argentina and Spain were followed up by another success which would leave the Scottish fans counting their money and plotting their way across the Atlantic. For there really is nothing like the World Cup for boosting not only Scottish football, but the whole country as well.

'The atmosphere's great. The players like rubbing shoulders with the best and the fans have rather come to expect it. It's not

What a season for Mo Johnston! Transferred from Partick Thistle to Watford, he played in a Wembley Cup final – and scored for Scotland as well

Scotland skipper Graeme Souness, who will be commuting to the World
Cup from his new home in Italy

that easy though. We have no divine right to be there. A lot of
countries bigger than Scotland have failed repeatedly,' adds
Stein. 'But I keep thinking back to that match against Brazil in
Seville in 1982 and I know that's the incentive to keep us all
working hard. That night it was a football occasion at its very
best.'

Just how far Scotland have to travel – and just how quickly –
was shown in that last match against France. While Scotland,
packing the midfield, never demonstrated any real cohesion,
France were playing with a verve and understanding which make
them so exciting. Michel Platini conducted an orchestra which
stroked the ball around to give the team a colossal amount of
possession with everyone else running into forward attacking
positions. By comparison Scotland looked pedestrian – or perhaps
jaded.

For, after all, it was the last match in a long season for many of
the players who had been involved in European as well as
domestic competitions. Why, Graeme Souness and Kenny
Dalglish were not even there, but away claiming Liverpool's

16

Sammy McIlroy thwarts Gordon Strachan as Northern Ireland beat
Scotland 2–0 at Windsor Park

fourth European Cup victory. When twenty-four hours later
England were dumped 2–0 by Russia at Wembley, with a dis-
gruntled crowd singing 'Come on You Reds', it did seem that the
plea of tiredness was a legitimate excuse rather than just a tame
apology. We really do play far too much football. The demands on
the top players increase all the time. And at the end of each
season, with freedom of contract in force, the minds of too many of
the stars are on whom they will be playing for the next season –
and for how much.

For the last twelve months, life has been difficult for the team
manager who consistently was unable, either through injury or
call-offs, to field his best team. And, in any case, how could you
expect players to get enthusiastic about the British Championship
games when the SFA had already decided that it did not want to
play Wales and Northern Ireland again. The truth seems to me to
be that, although it should still be the greatest honour in any
player's career to pull on the dark blue jersey, increasingly they
can't or don't want to psych themselves up for anything other
than the World Cup – and the game against England.

Jock Stein – facing the hardest challenge of a long career

Stein ended the season with a career record of 21 wins and 21 losses in the 53 games Scotland has played since he took over in the autumn of 1978 – middle of the road stuff. But it is worth remembering that he won the vital away games in the last World Cup qualifying group, the victories in Sweden and Israel being the most important.

Those apart, the away record is grim with only nine games won out of 29 played and three of those were against Canada, who hardly qualify as top-class opposition. He will need at least three or four points from the away games in this World Cup group if Scotland are to qualify, assuming that they can establish some kind of invincibility at Hampden Park.

In the end, it all comes down to the players. No-one could accuse Stein of not giving everyone a chance. In fact in those 53 games he has used 56 players, an awful lot and probably too many, even allowing for the fact that many of the changes were forced upon him after his original squads had been decimated.

Take for example the strikers. This is a list of the men used over the last six years – Mo Johnston, Steve Archibald, Mark McGhee, Davie Dodds, Alan Brazil, Kenny Dalglish, Derek Johnstone, Ian

Wallace, Frank McGarvey, Joe Jordan, Andy Gray, Charlie Nicholas and Paul Sturrock. In the last season he used eight of them, but only Dodds, Nicholas, Johnston and McGhee managed to get their names on the score-sheet with a single goal each.

Clearly, Stein needs to separate the wheat from the chaff, keep his fingers crossed that the injury jinx stays away and find a pool of eighteen who will be the backbone for the assault on Mexico. He admits as much when he says: 'We will have to slim the list down. In the last year or two we have given chances to a lot of younger players and we must decide which ones we need and which ones we don't as we start to get a settled side for the World Cup.'

This is how he sees the test.

Wales – 'They always give us hard games – and they were upset about the end of the British Championships. Ian Rush is a good spearhead for them, although he hasn't scored against us on three occasions.'

Spain – 'We were able to learn a lot about them in the European Championships. What is vital is that we beat them at Hampden Park and treat anything we might achieve in Spain as a bonus.'

Iceland – 'More than half their team now plays in Europe so they will have plenty of experience. And they are bound to take a point or two off the others. We must make certain that we are not the ones to suffer and, crucially, we must get off to a good start when we play them in the first match.'

My own opinion is that we can get through this qualifying section. Like the build up to 1978 which also had Wales in our group, the presence of two British teams is not in favour of the Spanish, who do not relish leaving the continental mainland. As France proved at the end of the season, Scotland may be some way adrift of the best countries in Europe, but that does not necessarily mean they cannot qualify.

SFA secretary Ernie Walker, in negotiating a new deal for the runners-up who will not now be involved in play-offs against other European teams but who will go into a straight knock out against, probably, New Zealand, Australia or Israel, also improved Scotland's chances. But Stein is quick to say: 'We don't want to think about creeping in the back door. We want to think about winning the group.'

Basically, I don't see many problems in putting together an adequate side, but one or two positions do cause some concern.

Above: Left-back was Scotland's problem position, but Arthur Albiston started to make it his own, here against Belgium

Opposite: An Old Firm international clash – Frank McGarvey and John McClelland

Where, for example, have all the great Scottish full-backs gone? Stein played out this last season with Richard Gough and Arthur Albiston, though patently Gough was out of form and Albiston still learning the international trade. Oh for Sandy Jardine and Danny McGrain to be available. It could well be in that position that Liverpool's Stevie Nichol and West Ham's Ray Stewart are the most skilful, but time, for both of them, is running short.

The rest of the defence, of course, picks itself with the Aberdeen trio of Leighton, McLeish and Miller the obvious choices – though I would not like to think that Alan Hansen, still the most creative in that area, has placed himself in permanent Scottish exile. Whoever Stein chooses, the defence should not leak too many goals.

In midfield the blend must be found. Graeme Souness still has his Scottish detractors although I can never understand why. He is the best passer of the ball in the game, is an inspiring leader and knows how to handle himself even in the toughest situations. But finding him partners is not quite so easy. Jim Bett is the most accomplished left-sided player while Gordon Strachan or Paul McStay should go on the other side. (My own choice would be Strachan, provided he is 100 per cent fit at the time.) Yet that leaves the midfield without what has come to be known as the 'ball winner'. Could Neale Cooper or Neil Simpson perform this role at the highest level? Only time will tell.

The scoring of goals is a much harder matter. If Charlie Nicholas had made the transition to English football effortlessly, I get the impression he would never have been out of Stein's plans. Kenny Dalglish, as well, cannot be written off – his last season was largely spoiled by a terrible cheek injury. Johnston and McGhee have done nothing wrong for Scotland. It is in this area that the manager must make the most difficult decisions – and come up with the goods. And one hopes, he will not forget a winger either – preferably Peter Weir, who can be so infuriatingly inconsistent but who does know how to turn defences.

Out of that little lot, there is more than the makings of a team. The 1983–84 season was so frustrating because on very few occasions was the manager able to make his final selections with all of those players available to him. At the outset of the World Cup, that should be less of a problem.

Jock Stein says we will qualify for the World Cup – and you won't find this fellow disagreeing with him.

You can't keep a good man down. Danny McGrain proving that there's a place for the over 30s

RANGERS' STORMY SEASON

Even by the bizarre standards of football, where yesterday's hero is tomorrow's villain, it was some story. For a month it wiped Mrs Thatcher and President Reagan off the front pages of the Scottish newspapers. It made Dallas seem pale in comparison. There was only one question – who would be the next manager of Rangers?

It started quietly one morning. When John Greig entered Ibrox on 28 October, there was no clue that he was about to set in motion a chain of events which were to lead the club into troubled times and embarrassment before the affair moved to that most satisfactory of conclusions, the happy ending.

It had not been a good time for Rangers. Their usual undivided support from the fans had begun to crack as the side struggled through the early stages of the season. No later than 17 September, with the campaign hardly under way, 300 fans gathered to protest outside the Stadium after a defeat by Aberdeen. More than double that number assembled the next month when they were beaten by Motherwell. 'Greig must go, Greig must go,' they chanted.

This was a massive breaking of ranks. No-one could ever find a bad word to say about Greig. He had given his all for the club for more than two decades, growing from a nervous young boy drafted into a club tour of Russia, to a mean full-back who had to carry the club through the lean years and eventually to a captain who helped win the European Cup Winners' Cup and clinch two trebles. He was Rangers through and through.

The trouble – as the general consensus afterwards stated – was that when Jock Wallace had left for Leicester City five years previously and Greig had suddenly been drafted from the dressing-room to the manager's chair, he lacked experience in that most demanding of all roles. Better, so said the expert judgement, that he had been farmed out for a while, just like Billy McNeill, who picked up invaluable experience at Clyde and Aberdeen

Ally McCoist, who forced his way into the Rangers side under new management

before returning, successfully, to Celtic Park.

He had, initially, brought Rangers a League Cup. Slowly he had replaced men like Sandy Jardine and Alex MacDonald, Tom Forsyth and Derek Johnstone, with whom he had shared so many triumphs. But the League Championship, the one title that really matters at Ibrox, had constantly eluded them. To the fans, the fact that it was two 'provincial' clubs, Aberdeen and Dundee United, who had come on so well, was especially galling.

Greig simply wasn't getting the results and the side simply wasn't playing to anywhere near its potential. In the law of the football jungle, someone had to go. Greig was showing the signs of strain – he looked older and tireder. The famous patter which had made him such a favourite was missing. He even admitted that he was shunning his weekly night out with his pals, and was even taking his wife out to dinner at six o'clock on a Saturday, 'before the restaurants start to fill up with other people.'

But the club showed an astonishing loyalty to him, testimony to the honourable way in which chairman Rae Simpson discharged his duties. He successfully defended Greig at an angry share-

Bobby Williamson, Jock Wallace's first major signing when the dust settled at Ibrox. The striker cost £100,000 from Clydebank

holders meeting. He would not sack the man he had helped appoint. That might be the way in other, lesser, clubs. It certainly wasn't the way that Rangers did business.

In the end, the decision was made by Greig himself, as it had to be. On Wednesday 27 October, Greig prepared to psych-up the team for a League Cup section decider against Hearts – which they won – and also put the finishing touches to the transfer of Jimmy Nicholl from Toronto to Ibrox. Outwardly, he seemed the same as usual. Inwardly, he had already decided to quit and told his family, who must have been glad the hard times were over.

At 9.30 the next morning, thirty Rangers players and staff were gathered together in a dressing room. Greig entered and tearfully told them that his Rangers days were over. He thanked every player individually. Then, still close to tears, he left. A huge weight had been taken off his shoulders. He went home and, before even the Press and TV stations had been alerted, was packing his bags and taking his wife and young son on a secret holiday, well out of the way of the prying cameras and the incessant telephone calls.

Ian Redford, who returned to favour under Wallace. But Alan Rough shows he remains one of the country's top keepers

They left behind a prepared statement in which Greig said: 'This is obviously a very sad day for me, as Rangers Football Club has been my whole life. I cannot leave without wishing Rangers and the supporters every success.' One of the best men in the game had gone. Thankfully, by the end of the season Greig had not only established a successful travel agency but was out and about round football again as a reporter for BBC Radio. There is no doubt he has recovered from those bruises – and will someone please be big enough to offer him a job in the game again?

The king is dead, long live the king. But king who? Rangers now had to go out and find a successor, knowing that their fans would settle for nothing except the best. It was the start of an embarrassing time, for with every move they made coming under intense scrutiny, they found it far harder to fill the position than they probably thought they would. For once, all Rangers power and influence didn't help – at least, not at first.

Alex Ferguson was the first and most popular choice. He had just brought Aberdeen that same Cup Winners' Cup that Rangers had brought home from Barcelona eleven years previously. The Dons, this early in the season, were on course for the championship. It was natural to think that a boy born in Govan, a former Rangers player, would find the temptation to return home irresistible. It was, in fact, eminently resistible.

Ferguson had conflicting loyalties to bear in mind. There was talk of a £250,000 contract in the pipeline. There were players at Pittodrie begging him to stay. There was the deep personal relationship he enjoyed with Dons' chairman, the elderly millionaire Dick Donald, to consider. There was his family as well. It was not a case of jumping into the car and racing south to the club which was his first love. All these things had to be considered. Rangers were still without a manager when they left for Portugal to play against Porto – they lost and went out of Europe.

It was there, in the Don Pedro Hotel, thirty miles outside the city, that the Rangers board discovered that Ferguson had turned them down. Disappointed, one director, Jack Gillespie, tried to hide his frustration by saying that there were 'dozens of people' who could manage Rangers. Of course, it was nonsense. Rangers were back to square one and time was pressing. If Rangers did not improve, they were heading for the inconceivable – a place in the bottom two of the Premier League and relegation. It was as serious as that.

Swede Robert Prytz, in and out of favour during the Rangers revolution

By the time Rangers left Portugal, the board seemed to be in a happier mood. Yes, they said, they had chosen their man. No, they couldn't name him at this stage. But it was no secret that it could be none other than Dundee United's Jim McLean, the man who had brought the championship to Tannadice the season before. As soon as they returned, the board mapped out their strategy to woo him to Ibrox and soon chairman Simpson was heading north to see his opposite number Johnstone Grant with a view to approaching McLean.

On the Friday, the Tannadice board decided that it had to let McLean speak to Rangers although they did not want him to go. But it was, after all, a once in a lifetime opportunity. McLean agreed to come to Glasgow on the Sunday, where he was offered a deal that no-one in the history of the Scottish game had ever come within touching distance of before. He listened for three hours as Rangers placed their cards on the table, one by one.

There would be a signing-on fee and fringe benefits which alone would have made him secure for the rest of his life. There was to be an annual salary of £70,000. Just as important to a singleminded person, there were two additional lures. He was to be his own boss, there would be no interference whatsoever from the board. Transfers, contracts, salaries would all be completely his own domain. And he could sign whomsoever he wanted, regardless of religion. McLean listened patiently and was obviously impressed by the generosity of Rangers, and the enormity of the challenge presented to him. He shook hands with Rae Simpson at the Ibrox door and said he would think about it.

He did and he didn't. When he walked into Tannadice on the Monday morning, he genuinely was undecided. Sometime in the next two hours, he made up his mind. He, like Ferguson, was staying where he was. Was it that he thought Rangers might be a bridge too far for him? Was he not convinced by those Rangers assurances? Was Ibrox too intimidating? In short was it a big business rather than the family shop he had run in Dundee? Did it lack 'soul'? Probably we will never know. Anyway the relieved Tannadice board offered McLean a testimonial and Rangers had now been turned down by the country's two top bosses. If it wasn't exactly a humiliation, it was at best a double setback. They couldn't afford to fail again.

By this time crazy names were being thrown in the ring. Tommy Docherty even got a mention. But it was clear that there was only one other man who had the stature and the experience to

Alex Totten, Jock Wallace's choice as his No. 2 at Ibrox

take on the job without being branded as 'third choice'. And luckily for Rangers there was absolutely no doubt that he would run barefoot the length of the country as soon as it was offered. Jock Wallace, the man who had brought Rangers two trebles, was at Motherwell – and itching to get back.

Why he had quit five years previously remains a mystery to this day. He had been a lifelong Rangers supporter and had been spotted for the job when he managed Berwick Rangers to victory over Rangers in the 1967 Scottish Cup. He had been groomed to step up as manager since joining Willie Waddell as coach at the start of the seventies. It seemed as though he would have his feet under the table for twenty years when he suddenly decided to go off to England and manage Leicester City. Subsequently, amid contractual wrangles, he returned to Motherwell – according to cynics to be nearer the two jobs he coveted – the boss's seat at Ibrox or the Scotland managership.

Rangers had no choice but to go looking towards Fir Park – but Wallace was under contract. At first Motherwell wouldn't let Rangers near him but eventually they conceded that there was no point in hanging on to a boss who wanted to be elsewhere. They did, however, insist that his outstanding contract be paid at a cost believed to be in the region of £120,000. Wallace was free to come home.

'Football's my religion,' he said in answer to the question of whether the assurances given to McLean applied to him. He was clearly gasping to get back in a much expanded role from the last time round. He outlined his plans with the vigour one has come to expect from the man who was a member of the King's Own Scottish Borderers in Malaya.

'When I go out for Rangers players, they will have to be desperate to wear that jersey, and they'll know what really hard work means. I honestly never thought I would get a chance to come back to Ibrox when I left, but my heart has always been here,' he said.

Soon the Wallace regime was in full swing. Rangers results improved and they went on to win the Scottish League Cup, the first sign that the corner had been turned. He went into the transfer market to sign Bobby Williamson from Clydebank and ended the season by taking Iain Ferguson from Dundee, proof that goals and plenty of them were uppermost in his mind. He took his side off on a round the world trip to Australia and Canada, convinced that the 1984–85 season would see Rangers climbing steadily to their 'rightful' position in the game, snuffing out the challenge of Aberdeen.

As I said, it was a story which had a happy ending. At the end of

Two players who couldn't reproduce their club form for Scotland —
Dundee United's Richard Gough and Rangers' Davie Cooper

the season, it looked quite like old times at Ibrox. But there were differences. John Paton had replaced Rae Simpson as the club chairman and there were very definite moves to make Rangers a more 'open' club, ready to explain its decisions. It looked as if they had finally cleared the decks for action.

Rangers' veteran goalkeeper Peter McCloy, whose performances earned
him a new contract which will keep him at Ibrox until he is over 40

WILLIE MILLER — FOOTBALLER OF THE YEAR

I was extremely lucky to be Footballer of the Year – lucky to be in a side of so many good players, lucky to be in a side which won both the Championship and the Cup, lucky to catch the eye of the Scottish Footballer Writers' Association sitting up in their Press Box and thinking that Willie Miller was their man. It wasn't always like that.

I started off, would you believe, as a goalkeeper. That's where they put me in my first games in primary school. They even picked me as a goalkeeper for the Glasgow Under-12 team to tour the United States. But if you have ever kept goal on Glasgow Green in the middle of winter, then you'll understand that the first ambition in football must be to get out of that position.

So when you get out of goal, it's natural that you want to play centre-forward, and that's where I was playing when Aberdeen first started looking at me. There were other clubs. I went down to Bristol City as a boy and they were in the First Division then. After that Celtic were interested in me. But eventually I signed up with the Dons. It is something that I have never regretted. But it was still a long time before I played as a sweeper.

In the reserves I wasn't scoring goals. It's a funny thing in a football club but when there are a rash of injuries, you don't think about your established position. If there's a game on, you'll play anywhere. The manager at that time was Jimmy Bonthrone and he thrust me into playing centre-half and that's how Willie Miller became a defender.

It became obvious that I was always going to struggle up front so I stayed back and that was clearly a turning point in my career. It just goes to show what part chance and luck plays in anyone's career.

That's why I say to any lad who asks me about taking up football professionally not to give it too much thought. The main thing when you are at school is to enjoy your football. Think of it as a dream, and also think of it as a very long hard road to the top. You've either got to be very gifted or very fortunate to make it to the top and I would put myself in the category of those who have

Willie Miller with just one of the trophies that ended up in his hands this season

been fortunate.

In the end if you are lucky enough to be offered a job, it's your attitude which counts. I see players in lower Leagues who were every bit as talented as me – in some cases more so – yet they have drifted out of top-class football and the reason is that their attitude wasn't right. They didn't hang in during the hard times. In football it's the same as anywhere else. Whatever you do in life, the more you put into it the more you get out of it.

I've never for one minute regretted coming to Aberdeen because in the eleven years I have been here, the club has been improving all the time. Remember, when I started we were in a period of Old Firm domination and the likes of Aberdeen and Dundee United were labelled as provincial clubs, good enough to give Rangers and Celtic a game and an occasional beating but certainly not strong enough to compete with them over a season. Now all that has changed round and I've been pleased to have a small part in it. Mostly it's been down to hard work.

I think three managers have done a great job at Pittodrie. Don't forget it was Ally MacLeod who brought us our first trophy – the

Footballer of the Year Willie Miller doing what he does best – guardian of his club's and country's defence

Scottish League Cup. His flamboyancy made us believe in ourselves and you could never take that away from Ally. And Billy McNeill carried that a step further. But most of what we have achieved has been under Fergie, who's a hard man to please.

I think we all had a hard time at first with him. He had to get to know us and we had to get to know him. But once we realized that he simply wouldn't settle for second best we began to understand each other. What it all boils down to is that if Fergie is certain that you are doing the best you can for him, then he's happy. That doesn't mean playing great stuff all the time, rather giving every ounce of effort you can. If you do that, there are no problems.

He works all hours of the day and night, seven days a week for Aberdeen and it's only reasonable that we match all that effort. And another thing he did was to keep his players and keep the team together. When I first came up here as a boy, Aberdeen had a super side but then they sold Joe Harper and Martin Buchan and the other lads lost a wee bit of heart. They wondered if it was all worthwhile.

Certainly we are going to miss Gordon Strachan and Mark

Aberdeen manager Alex Ferguson, who won the
Mackinley's Football Personality of the Year award
after his club won the double

McGhee. Mark, especially, has been underrated until last season
when he broke through with Scotland and scored that goal against
England. He does all the hard graft for us. The fact that the boss
once played him in, I think, twenty games when he didn't score
shows you how highly he rated him. He'll be missed.

So too will Gordon. He was the sort who could win games for
you on his own, he had the wee bit extra which the rest of us lack.
We will need players to replace them. Although the club has the
best set of youngsters in Scotland, you do need experience and I
think that whether we can hang on to the Championship or not
depends on how the new men settle in and adjust to the way the
club is run here.

On the international front, I look forward to having a chance to
get to the next World Cup. Spain was an eye-opener and there's
nothing like playing against the best in the world. Last season was
disappointing – I don't know why. We never had a settled team
and that didn't help. But I think that we have enough good
players around to do well, just as long as the manager is able to get
the side he wants onto the field.

THE OLD FIRM FINAL

Rangers 3 Celtic 2 (after extra time)

As a competition, the Scottish League Cup received a mauling from the critics this season. It had little shape, they said, being played partly in sections, partly by knock-out. And it seemed to go on forever. A complicated seeding system appeared to be designed less to keep the good sides apart, more to give the little clubs a chance to make money. When sportswriters have a white space to fill on a blank day for football, they return to such familiar subjects as winter breaks, summer football – and this time the League Cup. The criticism was valid. The League admitted as much when they changed the formula for this season.

Aberdeen manager Alex Ferguson branded the tournament a farce which was not only a strong attack but also delivered in the heat of the moment, after the Dons had gone out to Celtic in the semi-final. Yet almost all was forgiven after an enthralling final, and whatever the early flaws, the climax was compulsive.

In recent years, the New Firm has replaced the Old Firm. As Ferguson was to say at the end of the season when picking up the Mackinlays Football Personality of the Year trophy – beating his captain Willie Miller by a single vote – he looked forward to the time when Hearts, Hibs and Dundee would come to challenge even more strongly because, 'it would give us a great Premier League. It was never good that Rangers and Celtic should dominate the rest.' True, but there is nothing like an Old Firm Cup final, full-blooded, red raw, and that was what the final was all about on 25 March.

There was more than the usual incentive when the Old Firm met. Jock Wallace, after just four months back in the Ibrox job, wanted victory to prove that his immediate actions had been correct – and to give his supporters a fillip after two lean years. Celtic's Davie Hay was already on record as saying that he would quit if a trophy didn't end up at Parkhead, a statement he was subsequently to retract.

In all the propaganda that led up to the final, it was a good idea

to consult the bookmakers whose sober assessment of the odds is always a more realistic guide to the chances than all the old war cries. They had Celtic installed as the comfortable favourites, largely on the strength of the fact that Rangers preparation had been seriously disturbed by the events seven days previously. Then Dundee had not only brought to an end a twenty match unbeaten Rangers run but in the general furore Ian Redford and Robert Prytz had both been sent off and would miss the Hampden battle. On top of that the newly-signed goalkeeper, Nicky Walker, and striker Bobby Williamson were both ineligible. Rangers had gone off to play a friendly against Linfield as part of their preparations.

The final was on a Sunday, not much to the liking of some residents of Mount Florida who knew that their Sabbath was about to be disturbed by Rangers attempting to make sure they did not go trophyless for twenty-four months for the first time in thirty-two years. The crowd which eventually made its way to the ground was 66,369. They saw a game as interesting as any in the long-running series of what is justifiably called the greatest club

Opposite: On the way to the final – Tommy Burns tricks Kilmarnock's Jim Cockburn. Celtic won 1–0 at Rugby Park

Below: The Scottish League Cup final at Hampden Park. Ally McCoist miskicks while Davie Cooper tries to control the ball. Tom McAdam, Pat Bonner and Danny McGrain stand guard

game in the world. It took a long time to resolve – and the antics in both dug-outs showed just how desperate both sets of management were to win for their supporters.

For a long time Rangers were the masters, inspired by Robert Russell, whose return to form had coincided with Wallace returning to his old desk. At best, Russell is the very epitome of the old-fashioned inside-forward – up and back – and here he was at his very best. Paul McStay tried to match him, as a hard game – Reid was booked early on – needed someone to stand on the ball and play.

Something had to give and did so on the stroke of half time. Russell, who had bothered Celtic, sprinted into the penalty area and was cut down by MacLeod. Ally McCoist made an efficient job of the spot kick, slamming the ball inside Bonner's left-hand post. It was a little against the run of play but that's often the case when the Old Firm meet.

Ten minutes after half time, Rangers brought on the young Hugh Burns for John MacDonald and so one of the most promising youngsters in the Scottish game was going to feature in one of its big occasions. He had not been on long when Rangers extended their lead and scored their second goal which had its origins in goalkeeper Peter McCloy. His long-range kick has always suggested that he could singlehandedly put a satellite into orbit. This time, his enormous clearance was patrolled by Aitken, under pressure from Clark. The ball broke to McCoist, who confirmed that it was to be his day by shooting past Bonner. It looked like a canter for Rangers.

But after 67 minutes Rangers captain John McClelland was booked for fouling Tommy Burns on the edge of the penalty area. Burns took the kick himself, a delicate little chip over the wall and Brian McClair, that ever improving striker, volleyed past McCloy. Celtic were now very definitely back in the match and a whole rash of substitutions showed that the battle was far from over. Wallace was constantly up on the touchline urging Rangers on.

The next act of drama came almost on the whistle. Rangers were already beginning to celebrate as Celtic swept down the pitch again. MacLeod looked certain to score when McCoist, earlier the hero, became the instant villain when he pulled the legs from MacLeod. Mark Reid now faced the hardest task in sport – taking a penalty to keep his side alive in the Cup. He made no mistake and this hard game which had already seen six bookings, swept into extra time.

It was all decided by the third penalty of the game – and again McCoist was right in the middle of the action. He was brought

42

down by Roy Aitken, picked himself up, scored his second penalty and notched up his hat-trick to make it a final he would never forget. 'Actually Davie Cooper's our penalty taker,' he said afterwards. 'But I felt confident so I asked him if I could take it and he said "Go ahead". To score a hat-trick in a Cup final is a dream come true. There seemed to be some doubts about my future at Ibrox – but they are all resolved.'

Jock Wallace, his manager, said, 'When we were two up I was on cloud nine but all credit to Celtic, they fought back well. I thought Russell was outstanding, especially as he had to play in the same area as Tommy Burns, who did so much for his team.'

He cavorted with his players and the fans turned cartwheels on the terraces. It had been a match for strong men with the tackling frequently far too hard. But Rangers were back on the rails and those who hailed Wallace as a Messiah when he returned to Ibrox were proved correct. The machine was working again.

Peace and harmony before the final. Captains Danny McGrain and John McClelland

WHEN IN ROME...

You won't catch Jim McLean sitting down to a plate of spaghetti these days. If he ever decides to change his car, it certainly won't be a Fiat. And he won't be taking his holidays on the Adriatic. He's not too keen on the Italians these days.

Dundee United's season ended abruptly, suddenly and, according to the manager, unnecessarily in the heat of Rome's Olympic Stadium on 25 April. They arrived there with a place in the European Cup final waiting for them. They departed nursing their broken pride and knowing that their chance of what would have been real glory had disappeared. Even now the memory still pains the manager.

'We froze,' he says. 'We just didn't play. And the way the Italians behaved over both legs sickened me. It was sad to see a country which has so much to offer stoop so low. That's not an excuse. We were beaten fair and square on the pitch. But off it – that was a different matter.' The whole story of that semi-final is worth repeating as an object lesson to others who would claim the ultimate prize for any club, that massive trophy first handled by a Brit when Billy McNeill picked it up in Lisbon in 1967.

The draw against Roma was probably not the tie that United would have chosen. Were they not one of the richest clubs in the world, able to tempt Brazilian star Falcao to Europe at a salary of more than £500,000 a year? Did they not have the enormous incentive of knowing that if they won, the final itself would be played in front of their own supporters, 69,000 banner-waving Italians worth at least a goal of a start? And who were United?

In Roma's eyes, probably just a team of hicks from the sticks, their homely Tannadice looking like a prefab compared with their own mansion. United's entire wage bill might not even match Falcao's salary. They could hardly have expected the surprise

Maurice Malpas – here in action against Rangers – was the only man to be praised by manager Jim McLean as Dundee United slumped out of the European Cup

Substitute Tommy Coyne discovers that when Italians decide to defend,
there are no half measures

that was in store for them when they arrived on Tayside.

Since becoming champions the previous year, United had found the going tough. To an extent they had won the club's first flag because their slender first-team pool had managed for the most part not to get injured. This time, the constant chopping and changing had meant they had been unable to mount a really serious challenge. They were later to go out of the Cup against Aberdeen. So victory against Roma was essential if United's momentum was to continue.

McLean had built a remarkable team, mainly on the cheap. He had transformed United from mere provincials into a side respected all over Britain. As Lawrie McMenemy said, speaking at a testimonial dinner for the manager: 'Maybe you don't appreciate what this man has done. Sometimes when you are close to something, you can't see what it is. But from where I sit in Southampton, I can see that Jim has done a better job than any other manager in Britain. He has built a club from next to nothing. And you've no idea how much skill and how much damned hard work that takes.'

Still, even fervent Scots probably thought that United were the outsiders against the aristocrats before the first leg started. Ninety minutes later they had become the favourites. In a stunning display against an Italian side which was far more progressive than we had thought possible, United had gained the cushion of a two-goal lead. It was the greatest night ever for the 20,543 who packed Tannadice.

After a good first half, United took the lead magnificently in the forty-eighth minute. Ralph Milne and Davie Dodds set up the move to allow Eamonn Bannon to have a shot. That was blocked but the quick-thinking Paul Sturrock whipped the ball to Davie Dodds whose right foot shot put the Taysiders into the lead. That was followed on the hour by a 30 yard Derek Stark rocket which crashed into the back of the net. United held on and were worth no less than their two-goal lead. How to get to Rome was the only thought in the fans' minds.

But the sensations of the night were not over. Ten minutes after the game Roma made the incredible allegation that United's performance could not have been possible unless they were on drugs. The Scots, they alleged, had been on stimulants. It was laughable, of course, but according to McLean, no less than he expected.

Opposite: Footballer of the Year Willie Miller breaks up a Celtic attack. Goalkeeper Jim Leighton is there – but not needed

Above: Jim Bett who returned from Belgian club Lokeren to play for Scotland

Right: Up in the air at the last home international between Scotland and England

Below: Steve Archibald, loved or hated by the Scottish supporters, but always respected by defenders

Above: Davie Provan, hampered by injury, returned in time to take part in the Cup final

Left: Roy Aitken who ended the season with the unfortunate distinction of being only the second player sent off in a Scottish Cup final

Below: En route to goal – Mark McGhee

Above: Richard Gough gets his foot up in Tayside action

Opposite above left: Motherwell striker James Gillespie clashes with Hibs' William Jamieson during the Premier League match at Easter Road

Opposite above right: George McGeachie, Dundee, about to be tackled by Motherwell's John Gahagan

Opposite below: Henry Smith, Hearts' goalkeeper and one of the finds of the season

Opposite above: Rangers' Ally McCoist is not to be denied in an Old Firm clash

Opposite below: The goal opens up for Paul McStay in the League Cup final

Below: Paul Sturrock of Dundee United takes the ball past Celtic's Tommy Burns in great style

'They'd obviously had a shock. They might not have thought they could win, but they certainly didn't think they would lose two goals. And for me, it was obvious what they were trying to do – get themselves off the hook with their fans if they lost the second game, make us the villains and poison the atmosphere for the next match. They were just stirring it up.'

Still, United could afford the luxury of basking briefly in the glory. They had beaten one of Europe's finest sides. The doubts still persisted that if United lost an early goal in the Italian capital they would still be struggling against a Roma side which not only had Falcao (who missed the first game through injury) but also Bruno Conti, the teenager who had been a revelation in the World Cup final.

The Olympic Stadium is an intimidating place at the best of times. When McLean and his players arrived two weeks later, it was, as they say, a cauldron of hate. Banners in English hurled insults at McLean. As they walked out of the dressing-rooms they were pelted with oranges. It was obviously going to be a hard task.

'One of my faults as a manager,' says the dangerously honest McLean, 'is that I've probably never given the team the credit they deserve. Even when things have gone well I'm the sort of person who still picks out the bad points. What that has meant is that they probably lack a wee bit of arrogance, belief in themselves. But this time I was determined to build them up, to make the point that they had every right to be in this position and that there was no reason why they shouldn't win. If I had some innermost thoughts which told me differently, then I kept them to myself. I wouldn't have changed what I did for anything, but they still froze.'

Sadly, a glimpse of glory was shown to United early in the match when, from a Bannon cross, Ralph Milne crept up on the blindside to break clear. For Milne, it has not been the best of seasons. Normally he would have put the chance away to give his side a lead that even Roma might have found difficult to catch. This time he ballooned the ball over the bar.

And that, more or less, was about it. Urged on by a fanatical crowd, Roma found it indecently easy to get and keep possession. United chased shadows for the rest of the game. They were caught by a simple goal which should have been stopped, Conti's corner being headed in by Pruzzo. Before half time Pruzzo rounded the sad Richard Gough, another player nowhere near his best form, to shoot past McAlpine and the Italians were level. It was only a

Opposite: Tommy Burns holds off the challenge of Rangers' Dave McKinnon

matter of time and it happened in the fifty-seventh minute when Pruzzo, clear through, was tripped by the goalkeeper, and skipper di Bartolomi scored from the penalty spot. There could have been more.

As a final insult, Roma players chased McLean at the end of the match and the afternoon in the famous city was over. 'Only Maurice Malpas played,' bemoaned McLean.

The dream was over. It was back to the drawing-board with United reminded that, far as they had travelled, there was still a long road ahead. As some consolation it was Scot Graeme Souness who deprived Roma of the Cup when Liverpool beat them on penalties at season's end. But as a consolation prize, it was pretty small beer.

United gained a 2–0 win over AS Roma in the European Cup semi-final first leg at Tannadice. Here skipper Paul Hegarty goes close

50

ANDY'S LAUGH IN

'I did SAS training in the Glasgow Church League. We used to call it the Prison League. You should have seen the scars and the broken noses. Actually, they should have named it the Hospital League. That's where most of us ended up.'

Comedian Andy Cameron thinks that a lot of fun has gone out of the game. If that's so, it's not for the want of his trying. Football, and Rangers in particular, gives him endless streams of gags. Scotland's funniest man picks out some of his favourites.

'I can never understand why the English hooligans avoid the Hampden Park match. I'd have thought they would have enjoyed meeting up with our supporters. If they did come they wouldn't cause much damage – about thruppence worth. And that would only be if they dropped their empties.'

'People wonder why Aberdeen can't fill their ground. I mean, if Rangers and Celtic were playing as well as they are, Ibrox and Parkhead would be packed every week. Mind you, I know the answer. The ground's empty and there are 24,000 outside waiting for a lift over.'

'Big Jock Wallace had a hard time when he came back to Ibrox. The first morning he took all the first-team squad out onto the training pitch and said that he was going back to basics. "This," he said, "is a ball." Four of the team shouted back, "Hey boss, don't go so fast."'

'When Rangers won the League Cup, someone asked where the trophy room was. Big Jock got the key, opened the door and Shergar jumped out. That wasn't all. Lord Lucan was riding him.'

'This Scottish fan turns up at Euston on the way back from Wembley. The police ask him to open his suitcase and six foot of turf falls out. "'Ullo 'Ullo," says the policeman, "you've been on the pitch and taken that." "Not at all," replies our man. "My brother's away and I'm just minding his garden." '

From all that, you can gather that Andy has his hand on the pulse of Scottish football. He's a season ticket holder at Ibrox and rarely misses a game. He just wishes that the game was more fun.

'Take that Scottish Cup final for instance. I'd a lot of sympathy for Roy Aitken when he was sent off because there were others on both sides who had committed fouls just as bad and got away with them. But that sums up how it's changed. A Cup final used to be about both teams trying to play their very best football, shaking hands at the end with the losers saying "Well done" and knowing they had tried their hardest. It doesn't seem like that now.

'My favourite player of all time was Jimmy Millar. What I liked about him was that if the centre-half was bothering him unfairly, you'd never catch him bleating to the referee, looking for protection. He'd carry on playing and deal with the man in his own good time.

'The present players are good, but there's too much huffing and puffing. Too much of the Lion Rampant thing. We'd be a lot better if we cooled it. I like teams like that Scottish side at Wembley, men like Jim Baxter and wee Bobby Lennox and Denis Law. They just went about it their own way.

'Remember when we scored the goal against Brazil in the Spanish World Cup. We were going over the moon about it. It was as if we'd won the Cup. All the Brazilians did was roll up their sleeves and say to themselves "We'll need a couple now." And they got four.

'For all that it's still a great game. I was driving along the other day with George Mulholland, the guy from Scotstoun who emigrated to Canada and flies back for as many Rangers games as he can. We passed some school fields where the boys were practising cricket. I said to George, joking, "How about stopping for half an hour to watch?" George said, "Anybody who watches cricket would watch a dentist at work." No, there's not much wrong with the fitba'.'

THE TOWN THAT NEEDED GOOD NEWS

It was a year when the name of Scott Lithgow was rarely off the front page. That famous shipyard in Port Glasgow was dying. The streets of the town, and neighbouring Greenock, were black with men, even on weekdays, as the unemployed searched for something, anything, to do. If ever a place needed a smile, it was here and now.

Morton looked an unlikely football club to provide it. For five years they had been the phenomenon of the Premier Division, a club without the bankroll of the Big Four who could, nevertheless, survive with some ease among the elite. Largely that was due to the drive of its managerial pair Benny Rooney and Mike Jackson – and it owed a lot to the gypsy skills of Andy Ritchie, one of the last players to go about his business with a smile on his face.

The stories of Andy are legion. In bad weather, Morton train in

Even the loss of Alex Miller to neighbours St Mirren couldn't stop Morton's promotion drive

the corridor behind the main stand. One night, as the squad were doing sprints, Andy turned the lights off, leaving the whole team crashing into each other in the darkness. Another time, when a fan shouted from the terraces that it was time he broke sweat, Andy quipped back, 'Be quiet, can't you see there's some of us trying to get some sleep out here.' Morton, you see, was a happy club.

But by the start of the season, things had gone sour. The bank manager was not as friendly as usual. Players had always gone from Cappielow, men like Joe Jordan, bought by Leeds United for a bargain basement £15,000, and more recently, Bobby Thomson to Hibs and Joe McLaughlin to Chelsea. Now the demands of keeping a team had become even greater and it was decided that the club could no longer stand the cost of Rooney's wages (around £20,000) or those of his assistant, Jackson. Acrimoniously, the pair departed – Jackson was later to take his case successfully to an industrial tribunal.

Morton began the hunt for a successor. Willie Garner of Alloa Athletic, just about the most knowledgeable coach in the game was touted. Garner stayed at Alloa, eventually joining up with Alex Ferguson at Aberdeen and he remains my tip to become the outstanding manager of the 1990s. Eventually, the club's eyes turned to Alex Miller.

Miller had been many years at Ibrox, without ever establishing himself as an out-and-out first-team player. But all the time he had been studying the game. I remember once bumping into him at a deserted Glasgow cinema where we formed a matinee audience of two to watch a World Cup film. Of Miller, Jock Wallace says, 'There's no doubt that Squeakie will become a top manager, for one reason above all others. He works at it.'

He certainly had his work cut out at Cappielow. And early season results suggested that Morton's fight this season might be to stop passing straight through the First Division rather than challenging to get back into the Premier League. But slowly he began patching together a side. Crucially, he bought Raith Rovers goalkeeper Murray McDermott, an inspired signing if ever there was one. McDermott became Morton's Player of the Year and gave the defence a certainty which had been lacking in a poor League Cup section performance. Dougie Robertson, signed from Rangers turned out to be the League's leading goalscorer. Then there came a bombshell. After only a couple of months – important ones because Miller had turned the team round – St Mirren and Rikki McFarlane parted company. They looked no further than the near Renfrewshire neighbours for a replacement. They had noted Miller's work.

By this time, Morton were surging to the top of the League in

By the end of the season, Tommy McLean had also gone. But before he left for Motherwell, the first division trophy was at Cappielow

what was to become a three horse race with the fancied Partick Thistle and the unnoticed and unfancied Dumbarton. Morton kept their nerve, and allowed backroom boy Eddie Morrison, the former Kilmarnock and Morton striker, to take over the running of the side. He had eight games and Morton won the lot. No wonder at the end of the season, he was joking: 'Fancy that, the only unbeaten manager in Scotland.' But he wasn't keen to become the outright boss.

Fortunately, a replacement was at hand. Tommy Mclean had been forced out at Ibrox after all the upheavals there. A quiet, reserved sort of person – though underneath a man of steel – he came and brought with him his long-time pal, who had shared a room with him in Rangers' glory years and protected him on the park, Tom Forsyth. He managed to persuade Hearts to give him Willie Pettigrew on loan, a move which was later hardened into a £10,000 transfer and from that moment he had the core of the side which was to go on and win the championship.

It was, however, a triumph tinged with sadness. For years, Morton FC meant Hal Stewart. In February, playing golf at

Haggs Castle on a bitterly cold day, Hal had a heart attack and died. He was 77 – '77 going on 46' as Ian Paul wrote in the *Glasgow Herald*. It was an immense blow to the club and to the whole of Scottish football as well.

Hal had started life as a signalman in Dundee. He joined the Co-op and sold cigarettes. He became pally with the late Dundee manager George Anderson, who liked Hal's style. He was an upfront box-office character who knew the value of publicity long before football ever came to realize that it had to go out and sell itself. (Once he took Dundee to South Africa and they played in an all tartan strip, masquerading as a full Scottish side.) He had bought into Morton in the early sixties when they were on their uppers, persuaded a whole clutch of Danish players to come over and settle here and was known throughout the game as 'Mr Morton.'

Hal would do anything for the club. One of my favourite stories concerns the time when money was tight (when isn't it?) and half a dozen clubs got together to sort out a transfer which was more of a chain letter. Players would move around, cheques would follow them and everyone would be able to show the bank managers they were doing their best. At the end of it, the players would be back where they started. As soon as the chain reached Morton, Hal took the cheque, leaving the others furious but unable to do anything about it. He did all this with a smile on his face – and was much loved.

The night of his funeral, Morton, where hospitality is legendary, was silent as the side beat East Stirlingshire and moved even more strongly into the running for the title. The unspoken wish was that they should go on to top the League as a tribute to the man who had kept the club alive during the dark days, of which there were many. In this, they were helped by Partick Thistle, who simply fell apart.

That was the other major First Division story of the season. Thistle had a poor year. They were strapped for cash and in mid-season announced that they wanted to make manager Peter Cormack a part-time boss. He was not impressed but carried on. But the side simply collapsed, throwing away a seven point lead which allowed not only Morton but Dumbarton to pass them and go up. What went wrong? Possibly the board's lack of confidence in the manager communicated itself to the dressing-room but really a side with the likes of Alex O'Hara and Kenny Watson shouldn't have let that opportunity slip. By one of those funny ironies in football, at the end of the season the Jags appointed the same Rooney and Jackson as bosses, ending a year long exile out of the game. And everyone was duly pleased for that likeable pair.

'Will this be Thistle's year?' is the annual cry from the Jags supporters. Season 1984–5 should be and there's no doubt the Premier League would be that much better for their presence.

But back to Morton. They couldn't stop winning. It soon became a question of whether they or the Sons of the Rock would be crowned Champions. A good win over their rivals at Cappielow helped, and promotion was duly celebrated a couple of weeks before the end of the campaign. The roar from the dressing-room at Falkirk when news filtered through that the Jags had lost again, told its own story. Luckily Dom Sullivan, once of Celtic and Aberdeen and another good acquisition in mid-season, had a pub in Denny. Upstairs, they had a couple of drinks. Chairman Hugh Currie reminded the team that the championship was still the priority.

That was by no means cut and dried. Indeed on the last day, if Dumbarton had beaten Ayr and Morton lost at home, the flag would have been raised at Boghead. Scottish League president Davie Letham arrived at Cappielow but had arranged with the police for a fast car to take him over the Erskine Bridge if the results went that way. In the event, Morton scored three and even if Killie hit back with two late on, it was clear that the title was theirs.

'Please keep off the pitch at the end,' said the announcer, which was rather like King Canute ordering the waves into retreat. Hundreds of schoolboys – they had been let in free – invaded the pitch and enthusiasm and glory had returned to Cappielow. They were going back at the first attempt and it was a proud skipper, Jim Duffy, who held the trophy aloft. Behind the scenes in the boardroom, there was another ceremony taking place. Sir Eric Yarrow of the shipbuilding firm had commissioned a portrait of Hal Stewart. That was unveiled in front of his widow Laura and daughter Sylvia who admitted that she had been standing secretly on the terraces watching the club that her Dad built gain their way back into the elite.

Manager McLean took the congratulations quietly, Eddie Morrison admitted that he could throw away the threadbare suit which had become a badge of superstition and the curtain rang down merrily on the season. Hal would have loved it all.

SONS OF THE ROCK

Dumbarton general manager Alec Wright: 'Why we have every right to be in the Premier League.'

I was never more angry than when I heard people saying – and writing – that we had no place in the Premier League. I tell you something, we are not going up there just to make up the numbers. We're going to have a good go and if we do stay up and are successful, nothing would give me more satisfaction than to remind those who have written us off before we started that we have achieved our aim.

I mean, what more are we expected to do. We almost won the First Division. OK, we are not a big club, but you have to start somewhere. I remember in the first season of the Premier League, Dundee United avoided relegation by the skin of their teeth and now they are good enough to get into a European Cup semi-final. I'm not saying for one minute that Dumbarton starts from the same place as United, but there's got to be some provision in football for ambition, and over the years at Dumbarton, we've shown that we are not short of that.

When I came here twelve years ago, you entered the ground through a muddy car park to go into a rickety old wooden office The terraces were a mixture of ash and old railway sleepers. The pitch itself wasn't clever. This place was aptly named Boghead. And the side needed a bit of improving. Well, I reckon we have made advances on all those fronts and deserve to be where we are today.

Take the pitch. We must have spent £40,000 to £50,000 on that alone and it's not the mudheap it was. The car park is all tarmac, the terraces have been completely concreted and we have built a new stand. That's not what you would expect from a club which has no ambition and we've no intention of letting it stop at that. We're always on the look out for new improvements we can make.

On to greater things. Celtic's Tom McAdam was just one of the many Sons to depart for greener pastures . . .

. . . Murdo MacLeod was another

Of course it's hard. Our gates have gone as low as 2,000 but in the last weeks of the season we were getting 20,000 which just shows you the interest that is there if you can do decently well. That allowed us to pay the players' wages out of the gate receipts, rather than to rely on lotteries and the other fund-raising activities.

What we are trying to do in the Premier League is learn from other people's mistakes. A lot of clubs spent an awful lot of money upgrading their grounds to meet Safety Certificate standards which only apply if your attendance figures are over 10,000. So we are going to limit our gates to that level, and where necessary the games will be all-ticket. But in this day and age, how many times are you going to get more than 10,000, even against the big clubs? The police are happy with our arrangements.

What really annoyed me was that people were saying we had no right to be in the top ten because we were a part-time club. But does playing full-time change a bad player into a good player? I don't think so. And we've a great track record in finding good players down here.

In my time there was Colin McAdam, who went to Motherwell, and his brother Tom who went to Celtic. John Burke left us for Dundee United. We discovered Graeme Sharp, who scored a goal in the Wembley Cup final for Everton, and Ian Wallace, who played in the European Cup for Nottingham Forest. There was Murdo MacLeod who went to Celtic, Graeme Sinclair who did the same and guys like Brian Gallacher and Raymond Blair. That's a record second to none and we are very proud of it.

Of course, we had to sell them. Finance demanded that. It meant that we got in about £750,000 and that's made all the difference to us. And I can tell you that we have four or five young boys here who could be every bit as good. We wouldn't be scared of using them in the Premier League because we've worked on the principle that if he's good enough then he's old enough. Murdo MacLeod made his debut when he was 16. We carried him through the first season but by the time he was 17 he was a first-class, experienced player.

And we're not frightened to have a go for the best. A few years ago we made a serious bid for Johan Cruyff. Sean Fallon and I flew over to Amsterdam to try and persuade him to sign. The Press thought it was just a gimmick but we were serious.

We offered him £2,500 a week because we thought that he would attract that kind of audience. We waited five and a half hours for him but he never turned up. I tell you, when we came back the chairman really chewed us up, saying we should have kept chasing him until we got him. Maybe we should.

61

I'm under no apprehensions at all about playing in the Premier League. Off the field, I'm a wee bit nervous about trying to get in all the sponsorship and advertising money that we can. We know there are a lot of local firms who will support us, but we've got to leave no stone unturned to make sure we don't miss out on an opportunity.

I know the manager, Davie Wilson, would like another couple of players but we have to be careful. What got us promotion was enthusiasm and team spirit, which may not be fashionable qualities these days but they can go a long way in football. When we lost Billy Lamont as manager, I took over for a couple of games and it was a privilege to work with the team. They wanted to do everything properly and well. We gave a chance to striker Kenny Ashwood, who's never got his career off the ground, and he took it. We sold Joe Coyle to Airdrie for £13,000 and got him back on a free transfer. He was great. Honestly, Gandhi could have taken over as manager and we would still have got promoted because it was that kind of a team.

We've possibly had better players than those who won the promotion – but certainly we've never had a better team. And that's the way I want to keep it. We're realistic enough to know that we can't live with the really big boys but the Premier League isn't full of them. There are clubs with which we can think about being upsides with – and that will be our aim.

If we can do that, I won't forget how angry I was about being written off before we even started. Those kind of statements can kill enthusiasm. And that's what we are all about. It would be nice to prove everybody wrong.

DONNING THE CUP

It was the Scottish Cup final which should have had everything –
and very nearly did. But as 58,000 supporters left Hampden Park
empty, apart from the little and broken dreams, they were
pondering on what might have been. Somehow Aberdeen and
Celtic didn't quite get it right.

While at Wembley on the very same day, the FA Cup final
between Everton and Watford was decided in Merseyside's
favour by two Scots, Andy Gray and Graeme Sharp – a game
played largely without controversy, while 400 miles to the north
there was uproar and mayhem. There's no such thing as a quiet
game here.

One player sent off, an argument between a manager and a
referee at half time, and an official protest to the SFA at the end,
all show that Hampden Park wasn't the place to take your
nervous maiden aunt. This was red-blooded stuff from start to

A setback for the Dons – Paul McStay scores for Celtic

extra-time finish – but it has to be said that Aberdeen emerged as the rightful winners of the Cup for the third year in succession.

That was the prize on offer to them in the week leading up to the final. The championship won, the Dons could afford to collect themselves and become only the second club in the country, after Rangers, to have managed that feat. The grandeur of it can be seen by the fact that Celtic, even in those nine seasons in a row when they were flag winners, still found three Cups too much for them.

Aberdeen had problems in their build-up. Gordon Strachan, just a week before, decided that he was moving to Manchester United. Mark McGhee was rumoured to be on Hamburg's shopping list, correctly as it turned out. What would that affect have on the Dons? Precious little, as both played important parts in the triumph.

For Celtic it was neck or nothing. Earlier in the season manager Davie Hay had declared bluntly: 'If we don't win something, I'm going to pack it in.' He subsequently retracted that statement but it is a fact that for Celtic to go through a season with no silverware on the boardroom table is considered to be failure by supporters whose loyalty to the club – and attendance on the terraces – never wavers.

The day was perfect. The threatened rain stayed away on the Cup final parade as the long dry spell continued. The buses poured down the road, stopping at fish and chip shops where the recent addition of 15 percent VAT on carry-outs couldn't diminish the need to see the game on a full stomach. Aberdonians may have the reputation of making every penny a prisoner, but still 20,000 of them made the journey south to see if Alex Ferguson's team could add yet another trophy to the impressive list. The Celtic legions were there in force as Hay brought back Frank McGarvey and Davie Provan, who had both been arguing with him about money, for the final all Scotland – well, give or take the Rangers support – wanted to see.

Both had easy passages to the final, relatively speaking, although Aberdeen, after wins against Kilmarnock and Clyde, had to overcome the formidable obstacle of Dundee United, which they managed only after a replay and a Mark McGhee goal at Tannadice. Ian Porteous, one of those many fringe players who are the envy of other clubs, scored the opening goal of the semi-final against Dundee at Tynecastle and Strachan suitably embellished it to take the Dons to Hampden.

Mark McGhee carrying Aberdeen to the Cup – before leaving the Dons for a new career with SV Hamburg

Celtic started at Berwick, but didn't let any ghosts interfere with their passage there. East Fife, where Methil had got into a big tizzy just at the prospect, surrendered by six goals, as did Motherwell a round later. This was heady stuff and when Brian McClair and Paul McStay scored against St Mirren in the semi-final at Hampden it seemed that a poorish season could be redeemed by one last stand on 19 May.

The propaganda was considerable: 'I hear my players say they are the equal of any in the country. But they can't keep claiming that if they don't win something,' said Hay. 'I think the biggest advantage we have is experience at domestic, European and international level,' countered Ferguson. The stage had well and truly been set.

After all the pipe bands and mini-football that preceded a game, indeed a whole competition, imaginatively sponsored by the Scottish Health Education Group, referee Bob Valentine started the game with what was to be only the first of what seemed hundreds of piercing blasts on his whistle.

And for a time it seemed that it would be Celtic who would force the pace. Twice Murdo McLeod came close to scoring as the teams tested each other. A goal then would have put a different complexion on the game, but gradually Aberdeen, who had started quietly, began to assert themselves. They had packed the midfield so heavily that someone pointed out if this was a house, the inspectors would be paying a visit. Indeed they had named Dougie Bell and Derek Stark, both midfielders, as their substitutes, a clear indication of where Ferguson thought that the game would be won and lost.

And they scored, not without the first controversy, after 23 minutes. Strachan, who was to have a useful game without stamping his authority all over it, took a corner on the right and Alex McLeish rose for the header. It did not have much force and broke to Eric Black who looked offside as he hooked the ball past Pat Bonner. Certainly both Jock Wallace and Billy NcNeill, in their TV eyries, thought there was some doubt about it. Mr Valentine, checking with his linesmen, had none. Celtic were one goal down.

That was manageable. What happened next wasn't. The game had been played at a fast pace and soon tempers began to fray. The tackling had gone over the borderline between the legitimately hard and the unnecessarily coarse. And in the thirty-eighth minute, Roy Aitken blatantly body checked Mark McGhee as he ran through the Celtic half. It left Mr Valentine with an awkward decision. The foul was crude enough to warrant a sending off but then, in Cup finals, no-one wants to spoil the occasion. The referee took the strict, and very brave, view that Aitken should have first use of the showers, and he departed to the pavilion with players on both sides arguing strenuously with the referee and each other.

Celtic, of course, are never more dangerous than when they are a player short. They memorably won a championship when reduced to ten men in an Old Firm game against Rangers. If Ferguson knew that, then some of his players clearly didn't. Throughout the second half they played a tepid match, content to stay in their own half of the field for much of the time. And the quality of their passing deteriorated as well. It was almost as if they were inviting Celtic to equalize and take the game into extra time. Four minutes from the end they did just that when Graeme Sinclair, coming on as sub, joined up with Danny McGrain and Davie Provan to supply the marvellous young McStay with the chance he had been waiting for. Suddenly the Cup final, which had been moving at a sedate pace to its inevitable conclusion came alive again.

You would always bet on the side scoring late in the game to start favourites for extra time. But somehow Fergie managed to raise the morale of his players and throughout the additional thirty minutes, they clearly had the upper hand. The winner came after 98 minutes when Bell hit a thunderous shot on to the bar. Strachan picked up the loose ball, sighted McGhee at the far post and dropped the ball onto his right foot to allow the striker to volley home his last – and probably most important – goal for the club.

The half lap of honour was completed. Ferguson, who had not been impressed by the way Aberdeen had played in the previous Cup final and had said so, this time seemed contented – or maybe relieved. Anyway, the red-bedecked supporters drank in some more glory while Celtic were forced to accept that they had been beaten.

However a sense of injustice remained. Hay accused Ernie Walker, secretary of the SFA, of trying to influence the referee who had come into both dressing-rooms before the match saying that the organizers wanted a show-game. Rightly or wrongly, that was the headline news the following day. In the complicated system of bonuses paid by the sponsors, Celtic lost £3,750 of the £7,500 they were due because of the dismissal of Aitken and the bookings of MacLeod, McStay and McGrain. Aberdeen lost £2,250 of their £15,000 first prize because of cautions to Strachan, Black and Stewart McKimmie.

Those statistics tell their own story – and you can draw your own conclusions. Mr Valentine is the best referee in Scotland and his courage under fire is not to be doubted. He did the best he could. Perhaps the wisest comment was made by the old Aberdeen star Joe Harper, who said: 'That was the seventh meeting between the sides this season. That's far too much. What we got was not a Cup final, rather than just another Premier League match between the two teams.'

It was a good game. What it wasn't quite, was a classic Scottish Cup final.

Another step nearer. Peter Weir's shot hits the post in the 3–1 win at Kilmarnock

GOALKEEPERS AREN'T CRAZY

All goalkeepers are crazy, so the old legend goes. Even team-mates have occasionally looked askance at the men between the sticks. They play a separate game from the others. They are the last line of defence and sometimes the first objects of attack when a mistake costs money. They have to be quick-witted, extremely agile and it helps if they are thick-skinned as well.

Scottish goalkeepers have unfairly got themselves a bad name. Tommy Docherty treats them in the same way as Les Dawson uses his mother-in-law – as a suitable target for jokes. 'Scottish goalkeepers,' he says, 'are like daffodils, they only come out once a year.' Personally, I think that the Doc would do himself a favour if he laid off Scottish goalkeepers. The ghost of Frank Haffey has long been exorcized.

There are some good keepers in Scotland. Morton's Murray McDermott was a prime reason why his club will be returning to the Premier League. Alan Rough, displaced as Scotland's keeper, was still one of the reasons why Hibs can continue to enjoy life in the top League. St Mirren's Billy Thomson has his admirers. But most people would agree that Aberdeen's Jim Leighton is the country's No. 1. The amazing thing is that it all happened by accident.

'I was a pretty average centre-half for my school team at Paisley. Then one day, they picked me as a goalkeeper for the district team. To this day, I have no idea why. It must just have been a mistake. Anyway, in I went and I've never got out. So my career started by error.'

And what a career it is turning out to be. Already two Championship medals have come his way, three Scottish Cup medals and of course the European Cup Winners' Cup medal when Leighton withstood the might of Real Madrid with his Pittodrie colleagues. In that time, he has grown in stature from the novice protected to some extent by Willie Miller and Alex McLeish to the man who is his own master, able to give his own authority to the team.

The statistics prove it – in 39 matches this season, the opposi-

tion left the field empty-handed as Leighton gained that enormous number of shut-outs. 'Of course it's not just down to me. I think we have the best back four in the country in front of me and that helps,' he says modestly.

The rise of Scotland's international keeper was sure but steady. Once he had been put in goal he came to the attention of Eric Sorensen, the mast keeper who was at that stage in charge of Thistle. He had already picked up other tips from Danny Stevenson. 'It was obvious that going to Dalry where I could learn from Eric was the best move and he became my coach.

'In many ways keepers are neglected. Clubs just don't have specialist coaches – as the junior you tend to pick up the game from the senior guy around. When I got to Aberdeen Bobby Clark was a tremendous influence. Coaches tend to let the keepers get on with it themselves and learn the trade that way.

'Really, in coaching terms there's not a lot you can do, apart from keep playing all the time and gain experience. There are a few things you can simulate but mainly it's a case of picking it all

Opposite: Pat Bonner – another good season for Celtic

Below: Alan Rough – one big reason why Hibs are still in the Premier League

Opposite: The goalkeeper as peacemaker. St Mirren's (now Dundee United's) Billy Thomson keeps tempers cooll

Above: The sight Jim Leighton hates to see – Charlie Nicholas in full flight, homing in on goal, here against Belgium

up in games, learning the hard way, you might say.

'One of the biggest assets a goalkeeper needs is concentration and you have to work that out for yourself. I like to think of myself as the eleventh member of the side all the time. The ball might be down the other end of the park and it might be a dreich wet day but you just have to gee yourself up to stay in the game, to kick every ball. Then when you are called into action you should be ready.

'The most important quality a goalkeeper can have, the natural talent if you like, is to be a good handler of the ball. After all you are the only one in the team who is allowed to touch the ball – and you have to be pretty confident about your ability to catch and hang on to it.

'Where the experience comes in is weighing up angles, thinking about where to be positioned, when to come out for the ball and when to stay put. As I said, Eric was my first teacher and then Bobby came along. You had to admire him because he was eighteen years in the top-class game and you simply don't manage that if you don't have the quality which managers look for in a keeper – consistency. It's no use making two or three great saves and throwing all that good work away by letting in a soft one.

'Bobby impressed me as well because he was never flashy. Goalkeepers are a bit like referees – you shouldn't notice them all that much. There are continental keepers who like to make the easy save look harder than it really is – but the best keepers, in my opinion, are never flashy. They simply get on with their work. That's why I admired Bobby and also Pat Jennings, totally unflappable.'

Yet do all those criticisms of Scottish goalkeepers hurt?

'To be honest, yes. I don't think they are very fair. Certainly the English have two great keepers in Gordon Banks and Peter Shilton, but they seem to think that every English goalkeeper is superb and every Scottish one isn't. That's just not the case. Maybe it goes back to those nine goals that Frank Haffey let in at Wembley. For every mistake by Scottish goalkeepers, you could probably point to the same kind of error being made in England. So it hurts. You feel like you should have a go back at them but instead I concentrate on doing my best and making my play speak for itself.'

He regards Charlie Nicholas as his most dangerous opponent. 'He's so unpredictable. He can do the most incredible things and with either foot.'

He's a wee bit happier now that Andy Ritchie has dropped out of the limelight because Leighton was just one goalkeeper who could be on the wrong end of Andy's audacity.

But the truth is that Jim Leighton has grown up to take over as Scotland's automatic choice between the posts – and it seems he will be there to ram the English criticisms down their throats for years to come.

Jim Leighton, now the undisputed No. 1 goalkeeper in Scotland

FOOTBALL ON THE BONE

Jimmy Bone of Hearts at the age of thirty-something is a walking example of that old joke about the footballer who had more clubs than Jack Nicklaus. Retained for yet another season by the Edinburgh club to help guide the burgeoning career of his young fellow striker John Robertson, Bone is in a unique situation to assess the merits of those playing football up and down the Premier League.

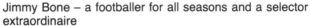

Jimmy Bone – a footballer for all seasons and a selector extraordinaire

Jimmy Bone in determined action

He won a League Cup medal with Partick Thistle in 1971 – curiously the first time the six-year-old Paul McStay ever saw his future club play. His pilgrimage took him on to Norwich, Sheffield United, Celtic, Arbroath, St Mirren, Toronto, Hong Kong and finally Hearts. His old head was invaluable at Tynecastle last season as he helped them to early points which were the mainstay of what was to become a successful assault for a European place.

I asked him if he would turn the clock back a few years to the time when the naming of a Scottish League side to play England was an annual talking point. That fixture has long since disappeared, but what, I wondered, would his choices be if he was manager and had to tackle picking the best team available from the Premier League. His selections will raise a few eyebrows for it wasn't always the obvious candidates who got the nod. He has left out certain Hearts players worthy of consideration – he didn't want to be accused of bias.

Billy Thomson (St Mirren) goalkeeper

I played over four years with Billy and he's got everything going for him. He looks the part and is terribly agile. People might be surprised that I pick him above Jim Leighton, another fine keeper, but I think that Billy is better on the cross balls. To an extent that isn't Leighton's fault because with such a good defence in front of him, he isn't expected to come for them. But Billy must – and he's good at it. No doubt the top goalkeeper in the country.

Billy Thomson shows the form that put him in Bone's team, ahead of Jim Leighton

Richard Gough (Dundee United) right-back
When I came to consider the team, I realized that there was a bit
of a dearth of full-backs. Richard deserves his place on merit but
there aren't too many good ones about. What I like about him is
that he always seems comfortable on the ball, which is the sure
sign of a good player. He's not afraid to go forward and is
comfortable there too. He has, after all, played in midfield. His
long balls out of defence are accurate and he's a useful man to
have around at the set pieces.

Alex McLeish and Willie Miller (Aberdeen) centre-backs
The choice was pretty easy here. You couldn't look past this pair.
And that's how you have to think of them – as a pair. As a striker,
you have to fight for every inch against them. They were already
outstanding before I went off for my spell in Hong Kong and I was
amazed that they had improved even on those standards when I
returned. Willie's grown in stature because he's acquired that bit
of arrogance to go on top of his skills at reading the game. Alex has
a lot more skill than people give him credit for and at 25 the
frightening thing is that he's going to get even better. As I say,
they are a pair, always talking and shouting encouragement and
advice to each other. When you score against them, it's a special
thrill.

Mark Reid (Celtic) left-back
This choice might surprise some people but for my money Mark is
simply the most improved player in any position in Scotland these
last twelve months. Like Richard Gough he gives the impression
of being comfortable on the ball. He can tackle and he packs a wee
bit of a punch that way. The measure of him was that he saw off
the challenge of Brian Whittaker, who was clearly bought to
replace him and who will now be joining us at Tynecastle. He likes
coming forward too.

Paul McStay (Celtic) right midfield
An obvious choice again. What amazes me is that here is a boy of
19, not being carried along by the older players but actually
running the whole side. There are games when he's never off the
ball and everything is going through him. He very rarely gives the
ball away, he's quick to spot an opening and he can be deadly with
his shooting inside the box. Look at the Cup final. I would have
loved to have seen him fifteen years ago when I started my career
and the marking wasn't so tight. Imagine him with more freedom
than you are given in the modern game. He would have been
hailed as the King – the new Jim Baxter.

Above: Up, up and away – Alex McLeish, almost an automatic choice for the team
Below: At the other end. McLeish and Miller show they can go forward, watching John Hewitt

Left: Paul Sturrock, hampered by injury last season, but still a striker who can make something out of nothing

Right: Ian Redford, a surprising choice for the team but a man Bone rates highly

Neale Cooper (Aberdeen) central midfield

Every side needs its Neale Cooper. Football is as much about winning the ball as playing with it. And every side can't be made up totally of the supremely gifted. It needs its workhorses, men to do the donkey work, and that's what he's good at. I don't mean he isn't skilful. In fact he is. The contribution he makes is that he will go and get the ball for you and if, say, a full-back makes a forward run, then he'll fill in there. He gives the others confidence to do their own thing. No wonder he's so highly respected by the other Aberdeen players – and the rest of us, come to that.

Ian Redford (Rangers) left midfield

Another choice might surprise a few people but you can put the kettle on for me as far as Ian is concerned. He gives you 90 minutes every match and he'll be up and down, up and down, like an old-fashioned wing-half. He really is seriously underrated. If I have a

Peter Weir, occasionally infuriating but on his day the best of that dwindling species, the winger

criticism, it is that he sometimes seems to have blinkers on. He'll work only his side of the park. But against that he has a lovely touch, can spot an opening and then be up on the edge of the box to accept it. A fair header too. I'd have no reservations about him being in my team.

Peter Weir (Aberdeen) winger
Any side needs a player who can go past defenders, and Peter does just that. But he does more. He has enough stamina on top of his pace to drop back and help in midfield when the occasion arises. As a six-footer he's better in the air than most. He won't score too many goals but, as we all know, he's one of the set piece experts, as good as you'll ever find. I chose him above Davie Cooper because he fits into an overall team plan better than Cooper. He's not just a winger, he's a man who accepts his responsibilities towards the team.

Paul Sturrock (Dundee United) striker

I know Paul didn't have a good season. He was unfortunate with injuries. But he's still the best at a new art created by the modern game. He can receive the ball and hold it until the rest of the attack arrives. That's not easy with the tackling. It annoys me to hear people say 'He's a manufactured player' as if there was something wrong with that. He's absorbed Jim McLean's teaching, he's gone to coaching classes at Largs. It's a pity a few more don't do that. Paul has taken in the advice given to him. If I had to fault him, I'd say that he would be a world beater with a little more devilment in him. But I didn't have any hesitation in putting him in the side.

Frank McAvennie (St Mirren) striker

He was virtually the first name I pencilled in. At 24 he's still not the finished article but when he is he will take some stopping. Basically, wherever you play him – he started in midfield – he will score goals. He's quick and he's brave and he'll score. You know, an odd point strikes me. He didn't get into senior football until he was 22 and Peter Weir was 21 when he joined St Mirren. I wonder if there is something in being a late starter. Maybe you retain more enthusiasm for the game. It's certainly a point to ponder.

That will start a few arguments but Bone runs his eye over the assembled team and says, 'It seems to me to have a good balance. The defence is tight and there's a bit of dig where it's needed. And there are left-sided and right-sided players. I really wouldn't mind looking after that lot myself. I'd even put myself on the bench and let them play.'

Frank McAvennie, one of the most exciting prospects in Scottish football

WHO'D BE A REF!

Even as he comes out of the tunnel at the start of the match, the booing starts. It will be the same at the end of the game. Like policemen, the referee's lot is not a happy one. He can be berated by managers and abused by players. Spectators treat him scornfully. He needs the hide of an elephant and his ability to shut his ears counts as well.

My favourite refereeing story concerns an Englishman called Jack Cambridge who was on the list for a while. Jack liked a joke more than most and one day as he ran the line in a match between Motherwell and Celtic, he was prepared for fun as he saw Ally MacLeod running towards him, nostrils flaring. He had just declared a Motherwell effort offside.

'It wasn't offside,' raged Ally. Jack reached for his yellow card. 'You can't book me for that,' snapped the manager. Jack con-

The finger of suspicion points at . . . who?

tinued writing on the back of his yellow card and handed it to Ally. On it was this message.

'Sorry, I can't hear you. I'm deaf,' it said.

Ally backed away apologizing profusely and returned to the dug-out where he was sitting next to John Hagart, who was his Fir Park assistant at the time. 'I'm terribly embarrassed,' he said to John. 'There I was shouting at that poor fellow and he's deaf.'

It happened that John knew Jack and said to Ally: 'No, he's not.' At that moment the linesman shouted into the dug-out: 'How are you John, good to see you.' Ally was suitably deflated.

It proves there can still be fun in the game – though precious little in the Premier League. I still remember one referee taking me to look at his dressing room after a match. The handle had been ripped off by a manager trying to break in to complain to the ref after a particularly turbulent game. Yet the fact is, praise be, that people still want to be whistlers and what would we do without them?

'I've had a lot of fun out of it,' says Davie Syme, one of Scotland's seven FIFA refs. 'I've been to places I would never have seen and been close to all the great players of the last decade. I was in the USA for four years running. Refereeing can bring you things that money can't buy.'

So how does any youngster who fancies being a man in black go about becoming a referee?

'In my own case,' adds Syme, 'it ran in the family. My father was a top referee. By the time I was 16 or 17 it became fairly obvious that I wasn't going to make it as a player yet I was still dead keen on the game, so it was natural that I should turn to officiating and I've never regretted it. Once a ref, always a ref.

'What a boy should do if he fancies taking it up is get in touch with the SFA. With more football being played at all levels than ever before, there's always a need for people to take charge. The SFA will put him in touch with his local association who will ask him for an interview. The only thing they will insist on is that he's not still playing. You have to make a clean break. A lot of lads would like to ref one week and play the next but the SFA is adamant that they do one or the other. You can see the reason why – you've got to be completely unbiased.

'In all probability, you'll be invited to take the referees' course. This lasts 12 weeks with two three-hour sessions per week and it's designed to make you familiar with the "Laws of the Game". At the end of it, you should know those Laws backwards. There's an exam at the end and between 75 per cent and 80 per cent pass it. But that's really only the start of becoming a ref. It's one thing to know the Laws, it's another to interpret them correctly and to take charge of a match.

'What's important there is self confidence. You've got to believe in yourself. We do get drop outs, we lose a third of all referees in the first couple of years. A lot of the failures are simply nice people who can't put up with players telling them they are wrong all the time. That's what the confidence bit is all about. You need courage to make a decision and stand by it, sure that you are correct.

'The real acid test of any referee is how he shapes up to difficult incidents in a game. I remember early on in my career reffing a Police match when I had to send three players in the same side off – they had been fighting with each other and I had no alternative. Eventually you have to rely on commonsense to take the heat out of the situation. You can either do it by being authoritarian or by being a bit of a humanist, crack a joke about it. It's really down to weighing up what is the best course of action to get the tempers calmed and the match under way again.

'As you get more experienced you should start to climb the ladder through the juveniles and the smaller leagues, graduating to the seniors. I always advise refs to carry on because the rewards – I don't mean money ones – are considerable. The seven FIFA referees frequently travel abroad – I've had 32 foreign appointments in 24 different countries and every time I've taken two linesmen with me. So you can see that there is a chance for a lot of officials to take big matches.

'My own highlights would have to be the Scottish Cup final in 1983 between Rangers and Aberdeen, as well as the Old Firm League Cup final in 1977, for getting the big domestic games is still more of a thrill than any European appointments. But the 1982 European Cup semi-final between Bayern Munich and CSKA Sofia in the Olympic Stadium stands out as well.

'And you get to meet the stars. There's no-one in my book like Franz Beckenbauer. I refereed him a lot in the States. He could stroll through a game and still be a class above anyone else. And no trouble to a referee either. Then there's Johan Cruyff and Karl Heinz Rumminege as well. A host of players who it's been a privilege to be on the same field with. I've no regrets about taking up refereeing at all – and I've still got another 11 years, potentially, on the list. We are not as bad as we're made out to be, you know.'

WILLIE ORMOND

William Esplin Ormond, whose death last season saddened not only the whole of Scottish football but also sent the town of Musselburgh into deep mourning, was the last of the great old-fashioned managers. Where others used fancy jargon, he preferred plain speaking. Where others surrounded the game with deep mystery, he kept it simple. He was also one of the great raconteurs. They buried a whole chunk of football history that sad day in May.

My favourite story of his concerns the first time he broke his leg. He was but a young apprentice with Hibs, learning the trade that

Willie Ormond, loved by all in Scottish football, who died last season

was soon to make him a member of the most exclusive club in Scottish football, the Famous Five. In the reserves, he was up against a grizzled old veteran from East Fife whom he proceeded to lead a merry dance. The full-back turned to him and said, 'Look, son, beat me fair and square and I've no complaint. Try and make me look a mug and then I'll have to take care of you.' The next time Willie got the ball, he beat his man, checked back and tried to beat him again. The next thing Willie knew was that he was lying on the track with his leg in two pieces. 'But the funny thing about it was,' he said, 'all I could hear was a voice in the enclosure. It was my Dad and he was shouting, "Serves you right, you silly wee so-and-so."'

If you understood that, you understood Willie's view of the game. He was a great player and a great judge of other players. It may look obvious now, but when he chose Scottish players like Jim Holton, Hutchison, Bruce Rioch and Don Masson, he was backing his own judgement rather than going along with fashionable thinking. The results paid off.

His favourite word was blend. 'Good teams have it and bad teams don't,' a fact as true today as it ever was. Once I ran a newspaper competition designed to allow readers to pick their all-time Scotland XI. Entries poured in in their thousands and I had to find someone who could judge them. I invited Willie out to lunch to see if he would adjudicate.

A lot of managers might have refused. What is good fun to the punters is often anathema to the professionals. But Willie agreed and I gave him a sheet of foolscap, saying that if we got it over with, we could then proceed to the serious business of enjoying the Dover sole. 'It's not as easy as that,' said Willie and three hours later he was still trying to find out the perfect blend. Could Baxter play in the same side as Bremner? Who should be Alan Morton's inside-forward partner? Was Denis Law a perfect foil for Laurie Reilly? It was typical of the man's attention to detail.

He remains, statistically, Scotland's most successful manager. He was certainly the wittiest. I'll long remember being in the gents toilet at Frankfurt's Wald Stadium during the 1974 World Cup when who should enter but Willie and the then Prime Minister Harold Wilson. The PM, who always carried in his wallet a picture of the Huddersfield side of his childhood, fancied himself as a bit of a football know-all. He said to Willie that he thought he was playing Peter Lorimer out of position, to which the manager replied: 'You get on with your job and leave me to get on with mine.'

He hadn't a bad word to say about anyone and was always bitterly disappointed when someone let him down. He could not believe that if he treated his players like grown men, they would behave badly. Occasionally they did and everyone remembers the famous rowing boat incident at Largs in 1974 when Jimmy Johnstone attempted a singlehanded Atlantic crossing on the eve of the England game. But Willie was a psychologist too. He picked the wee man for the game, despite all the bad publicity he was receiving in the press. 'Just you go out and prove them wrong,' Willie told him. Jinky did and the rest is history.

He was always nervous about Scotland. He wasn't averse to a drop of brandy before a game to calm him down and gradually it emerged that the manager was not only a good manager but a deep and sincere patriot as well. Scotland mattered to him very much indeed. That makes his considerable achievements even more impressive.

The afternoon that Scotland were held to a draw by Yugoslavia and became the first side to be knocked out of a World Cup without losing a match, Willie was in tears. So too was his wife Margaret. But he was much cheered up when the fans outside the ground started singing, 'We're on our way to Argentina, we shall not be moved.' That night he perked up and was the life and soul of the party and that's the way we should remember him.

The SFA treated him badly. Two years later there were moves to have him sacked. Getting wind of this the Press mounted a campaign on his behalf and I shall long remember too the time when we were returning in the plane from a good draw in Rumania, spontaneously, the pressmen started singing, 'If you like Willie Ormond, clap your hands.' That shamed the SFA into giving him a stay of execution but it was never quite the same for Willie after that episode. He left to go and manage Hearts and a romantic period in Scottish football was over. Argentina – and all that mess – followed.

So when they laid him to rest, it was the saddest day of this and many other seasons.

ALMOST A HAPPY ENDING

They came as always wearing enough tartan to cover Glencoe, enough banners to stretch from Gretna to John O'Groats. Those football insiders who insist that the game between Scotland and England, shunted into the cul de sac of the season, doesn't matter as much these days clearly haven't got the message through to those who really count – the fans whose search for tickets outdoes anything that happened on Treasure Island.

This was, ultimately, a sad game. The quietness of the 73,064 crowd who made their way in silence to the exits, emphasized that a draw in this fixture suits everyone and no-one. But it was appropriate that the last ever fixture in the British Championships should finish in an atmosphere that was slightly funereal.

The decision to banish Wales and Northern Ireland had been fiercely debated throughout the season. The SFA was rather put out by those of us who thought that at best it was unfair on our neighbours, at worst an act of treachery towards our friends. Money talks, of course, and it clearly didn't suit Scotland or England to use up valuable dates in a crowded calendar with games whose revenue earning powers tend to bring in little more than loose change. Nevertheless, it did seem to me wrong that we should deny the junior partners in football's oldest championship the right to make some cash, even at our expense.

Already there is talk that Scotland and England will this season be joined by one of the world's footballing superpowers in a three nation tournament to replace the Home Internationals. It may make some sense to invite, for example, West Germany to make up the numbers but where is the tradition in all that? No doubt supporters may prefer that to watching Wales or the Irish – but why throw history out of the window just to make a few more bob? It would be more sensible if the SFA and the Scottish League could sit round a table and re-organize a fixture list which left

Davie Cooper turns on the style during Scotland's 2–1 win over Wales at Hampden

90

room for both competitions. But resolving the differences between their own vested interests always makes it look as if Mr Arthur Scargill and Mr Ian McGregor are just about on the same wavelength. So as we watched the one hundred and second – and last – championship match between the biggest UK countries, there was time to pause and say thank-you to the Peter Dohertys, the George Bests, the John Charles and the Ivor Allchurches, who gave so much down the years.

The decline of the British Championship can be dated to the decision to shunt them into the end of the season. The optimistic hope that by devoting a week to them would concentrate interest was well founded, but overtaken by events. Players were understandably stale – they are human after all and want their holidays like the rest of us. The continuing success of British teams in European club competitions meant, over the years, that often the matches were played by depleted sides. In this last match, Scotland were without Kenny Dalglish and Graeme Souness, waiting to play for Liverpool against Roma in the Champions' final. Poor England, through a variety of reasons, were left with what wasn't much more than a second string side.

Yet the fixture remains something special. 'There's nothing like coming up on the train, packed with you Scots,' said an English pal of mine. 'Six hours and they talk about nothing apart from football. Then when you get out at Central Station, the programmes are on sale. It's the only city in the world where that happens and you think to yourself that football captivates the whole place.' He's right and once again, it is the supporters who make the magic possible.

Actually, this year I was a bit worried. One of the great myths about sportswriters is that they can put their hands on at least 100 centre stand tickets each. The reality is different – we have to scramble about like the rest of the citizenry to try and help out our friends. Normally, in the week before the English match we like to take the telephone off the hook and stay away from any place where there might be a ticketless fan. This time, it seemed that demand was limited, despite the cut in Hampden's capacity while rebuilding work continues. But by the Wednesday, long lost friends were coming out of the woodwork, all asking the same question – 'What about some briefs?'

It was clear that even a dull international season could not quench their ardour. They were to descend to see, amongst other things, whether Scotland, in this last championship match, would square the series against England, by making it 40 wins apiece with 22 draws. Or maybe they weren't taking any notice of that statistic at all; maybe they were just coming to give England a reminder that when it comes to football, the heart of the Empire still lies in Scotland. Anyway, everyone from Rod Stewart and his new girlfriend to half of Stornoway was there.

I had gone down to the plush Turnberry Hotel on the Saturday morning to interview Gordon Strachan for 'On the Ball'. Breakfasting with Jock Stein, I said, half jokingly, that I trusted the lads would all be briefed to get wired into the English. He chided me severely. 'No, it's not got to be like that. It's got to be about playing football, not about kicking people. We'd like to think that we could match England and then go on to play better football than they could.' That was the manager's hope. To an extent, it worked out that way – there was none of the feuding which had marred the Scottish Cup final on this same Hampden Park pitch seven days previously. But the conclusion was almost, but not quite, right.

The English, meanwhile, were at sixes and sevens. Bobby Robson was having a fall-out with the English Press up the coast at Troon and there was general amazement at his team. Deprived among others of Paul Mariner, Trevor Francis and Glenn Hoddle, no-one would have been surprised if he had fielded a side of honest toilers. After all, as late as the Thursday, he was saying, 'If I had to pick a team now, I just couldn't do it.' Instead he took the sort of gamble that would have given Sir Alf Ramsay nightmares.

He decided on two wingers, Mark Chamberlain and John Barnes. He concluded that Bryan Robson and Ray Wilkins could run the midfield by themselves and altogether he gave the impression that he, like Scotland's manager, was flying in the face of modern convention to give the fans the sort of game they like. Scotland were picked on orthodox lines, the only possible surprise being that Steve Archibald, after the UEFA Cup final between Tottenham Hotspur and Anderlecht, was preferred to either Charlie Nicholas or the prodigious Watford and former Partick Thistle goalscorer, Maurice Johnston.

Much was expected of Davie Cooper, first capped back in 1979 but due to play only his fifth Scottish game. Would his impishness and cheek turn the scales? Would he live up to a remark Trevor Brooking had made a few days earlier that he was one 'of the best players I have ever seen anywhere'? Scattered heavy showers replaced the sunny calm that had hung over Scotland for weeks. That, too, was an omen.

It started well for Scotland. After just 18 minutes of sparring they were ahead, with Strachan showing why he is worth £500,000 to Manchester United. He feinted to play the ball out to the wing, turned inside and crossed to the far post. It looked like a defender's ball but Steve Fenwick misjudged it. Mark McGhee, coming up on the blindside, hit a fine header which was placed down and away from Peter Shilton's despairing grasp.

How the banners flew. How Hampden roared for this was the first goal scored against the English on this famous ground for eight years. Scotland looked settled and skilful but that fatal flaw which has haunted us down the years cropped up again. Having got their opponents on the ropes, there was a decided reluctance to apply the knock-out blow. Instead it was England, with Barnes and Chamberlain worrying Gough and Albiston, who started to string their passes together, find their men and began to relish the running. Instead of forging ahead, Scotland were merely holding on.

Willie Miller, for once, was not that certain and assured defender who had carried all before him for the last ten months. And eight minutes before half time, when Chamberlain kept the ball in well and released Woodcock, he looked distinctly fragile. The striker wrong-footed him so completely that Miller was forced to turn his back on him. Before he had time to recover, Woodcock hit a left-foot shot of such wondrous power that Leighton could hardly have seen it, let alone got a finger to it. England were back in the match with a vengeance.

Scotland lived dangerously at the start of the second half, but gradually recovered enough composure to mount a rally. Much of their later strength was founded on substitutions which were the centre of some controversy. When Paul McStay and Mo Johnston emerged, they gave the Scots an instant fifth gear but not everybody was sure the manager had made the right decision when he pulled off the instigator and finisher of the opening goal. Strachan had done well and Robson admitted that he was surprised by the move of his counterpart. Steve Archibald seemed a more suitable candidate for the bench than McGhee.

Stein explained later: 'Our players knew I would make substitutions. We discussed that at Turnberry. Strachan did very well but I felt that he was beginning to get bogged down a bit. McGhee had done his bit in wearing down the English defence so we knew the replacements would benefit from that hard work. And I feel that Strachan and McStay are too similar to play in the same side. You don't make a substitution for the fun of it.'

Anyway, Scotland woke up. Johnston, in only his second international, looked like a player born to wear the dark blue jersey. McStay's passes were telling. They came within an inch of making Stein's decisions look as clever as anything Svengali ever did – but a remarkable man stood in their way.

Down the years, Scotland have not allowed football's fiercest rivalry to blind them to the fact that England can produce good

John Wark says 'After you' as Gordon Strachan tries to beat England on his own. It was just beyond him this time

players. They have thrilled to the likes of Matthews and Edwards and Charlton, accepting them as worthy foes. To that short list must be added the name of Shilton, who, not for the first time, denied Scotland victory. Johnston's volley, seven minutes from the end, would have beaten almost any keeper in the world, but the Englishman threw himself across the goalline, pushed out his arm, and deflected the shot wide. The only player on the field who could legitimately claim to be worth a place in a World XI, in that moment effectively denied Scotland victory.

The crowd stayed to the end. Alex McLeish had another late try, only to see the same Shilton save on his knees. It had been an open, fluent match with only one booking – Arthur Albiston for a series of fouls on Chamberlain. The Italian referee Paulo Casarin had an easy match, full of authority exercised unobtrusively. In the end the draw was frustrating – as they always are – but eminently fair. The crowd drifted away pondering how they would explain to their loved ones why they were so late home. After all, there was neither a celebration nor a wake to attend.

FINAL WHISTLE

I've enjoyed writing this book – I just hope you have enjoyed reading it. My thanks go not only to all those who have helped me compile it – but to everyone connected with the greatest game of all.

I'll leave you with a couple of my favourite – true – football stories because they seem to sum up the attitude of the Scot to his football. The real supporter simply can't be matched anywhere in the world.

When in 1967, Celtic had won the European Cup, Jock Stein went on to Nuremberg to see if Rangers could complete an historic double for Glasgow by winning the Cup Winners' Cup. As he approached the stadium, he bumped into a supporter wearing nothing except a pair of jeans and a scarf. That might have been all right on a Spanish beach but the trouble was that it was cold and raining stair-rods. The Big Man asked why he hadn't brought a coat.

'It wasn't raining when I left Glasgow,' the guy replied.

Or that other time when I was standing on the Firhill terraces and the man in front of me kept shouting that Doug Somner, who played for the Jags in those days, was a balloon. It kept being repeated every other minute.

Eventually, I leaned across and said that although he was entitled to his opinion, I should point out that Somner had been hurt in training and was not playing.

'Sorry son,' he said. 'But I lost my glasses yesterday and I can't really see the pitch.'

I should have known better and left it at that but I asked him why, if he couldn't see the game, had he bothered to come. 'Son,' he said, 'I haven't missed a match in 13 years.'

As Andy Cameron is fond of saying: 'That'll do me.' This book is not so much a paying of homage to heroes but more a tribute to those people who, week in week out, keep Scottish football alive and healthy. The fans.